# Eilean Dubh

## – The Black Isle –

Andrew Dowsett, James A Moore and Russell Tu~~rner~~

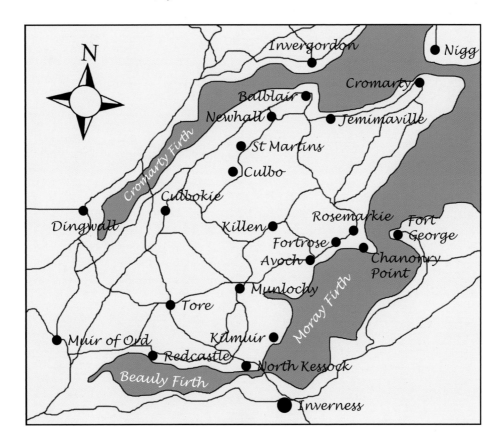

Bassman Books

Published by Bassman Books, Burnside Cottage, Newhall, Balblair, Dingwall, IV7 8LT

First published in 2010

Third (revised) edition, published in 2011

A catalogue record for this book is available from the British Library

ISBN 978-0-9567908-0-4

Printed by Big Sky, The Press Building, 305 The Park, Findhorn, Forres, IV36 3TE

Layout and design by Russell Turner

Photographed, printed and published in Scotland

*In memory of Ingy and with love and thanks to an amazing family who put up with me on a daily basis*

*

*For Celina – there could never be another*

*

*To Naomi, Ken and Richard*

Cover Page: Jemimaville and Udale Bay
This Page: Taking a stroll, Newhall

# Contents

Morning mist at Poyntzfield Mains

# Our Black Isle

THE most difficult part of compiling this book was deciding what to leave out. The Black Isle – Eilean Dubh in Gaelic – offers so many choices of subject, so many viewpoints, and such an ever-changing variety of light that the book could have been ten times its size and not include all we wanted.

If we've ignored your favourite view, or rushed past the village or hamlet where you live, we apologise. And if you were hoping to discover where the name Black Isle comes from, that's an old mystery – we certainly don't know.

What we do know is that the Black Isle is a beautiful part of the Highlands that deserves much wider recognition.

Take a look through the pages that follow and you'll understand why.

Left: Old Steading near Alnessferry
Above: Sunset, Millbuie Forest

# The Light

CHANGING light and seasons mean nothing is constant on the Black Isle. What never changes is the beauty of the landscape, whether clothed in spring colour, summer sunlight, autumn mist or winter frost.

Left: Farness and Udale, above Jemimaville, seen across Cromarty Firth
Above: Newhall Bridge post box

Migrating geese at sunrise, Cromarty Firth

A moody morning near Balblair

Oil seed rape fields, Rosehaugh Estate (left), and beside Munlochy Bay

Ben Wyvis and Cromarty Firth

Castle Craig, former home of the Bishops of Ross

Left: Autumnal
lane near
Munlochy at
Drumsmittal
junction
Right: Newhall
Burn

Evening on the Cromarty Firth

Balblair Slipway

Kessock Bridge (above) and
Cromarty Bridge, which carry
the main road through the Black
Isle from the south and the north

# The Villages

THE Black Isle was as isolated as an island until 1977, when Cromarty Bridge was completed. Kessock Bridge opened five years later and, for the first time, travellers from Inverness were able to reach the peninsula in minutes.

The ferry crossing from South Kessock or the long road journey via Beauly and Muir of Ord are becoming distant memories but the Black Isle retains pockets of untouched charm lost by many other areas of the Highlands.

Although development has taken place – particularly in recent years as Inverness boomed – it is not difficult to picture the Black Isle's villages as they were in quieter times, when most residents were employed in agriculture or fishing and motor vehicles were an undreamed of luxury.

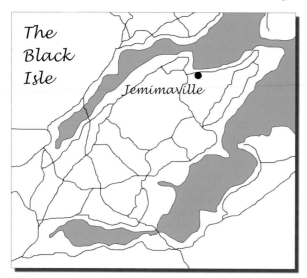

The Black Isle

Jemimaville

Winter frosts, Jemimaville

Jemimaville and Udale Bay,
an RSPB reserve

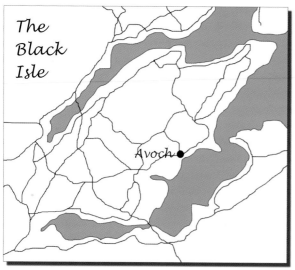

The
Black
Isle

Avoch

Above: George
Street, Avoch
Right: Avoch Bay

Above: Shore Street
Below: Monument, High Street
Right: Avoch Harbour

Above: Harbour reflections
Left: Avoch Parish Church
Right: Avoch Burn and Henrietta Bridge

Left: Rosemarkie Beach
Above: High Street
Right: Rosemarkie and
Chanonry Point

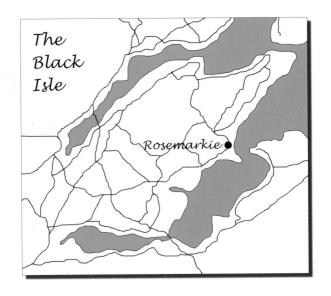

The
Black
Isle

Rosemarkie

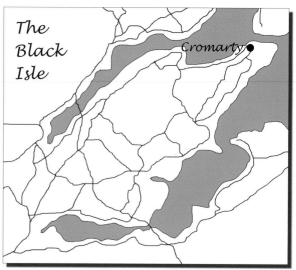

Above: Gordon's Lane
Right: Cromarty
Courthouse and village

Above: Cromarty seen from the South Sutor; Top right: Gordon's Lane
Far right: High Street; Right: Hugh Miller's Cottage

*Page 36*

Rain and shine in Cromarty

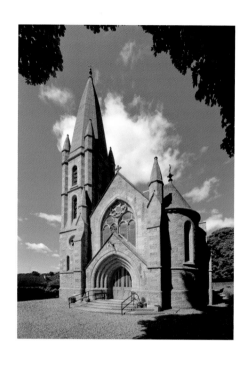

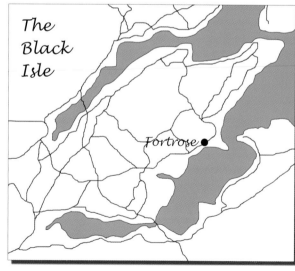

The
Black
Isle

Fortrose●

Far left: Fortrose Town House
Left: Fortrose Church of Scotland
Above: Fortrose Cathedral

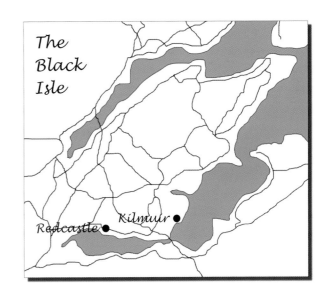

The Black Isle

Redcastle • Kilmuir •

Left: Kilmuir and Ord Hill
Above: Redcastle ruins

# The Land

A GRICULTURE and forestry provide a livelihood for many Black Isle workers and a habitat for domestic and wild animals.

The land displays beauty in every season, but the golden hues of autumn and the dramatic monochrome landscapes of winter are hard to beat.

Above: Highland cattle, Glenurquhart Farm
Right: Allangrange Mains near Munlochy

Out in the fields:
Above
McFarquhar's
Bed (left) and
Poyntzfield
Mains

Young heifers, Tore

St Martins and Ben Wyvis

*Page 49*

FRESH FARM
VEG

FOR SALE HERE!

NEW POTATOES (PREMIER)    £1 PER BOWL
                          3 scoops for £2
SUMMER CABBAGE            50p each
BROCCOLI                  £1 for 3 heads
BEANS                     20p per spray
BEANS AND SOME MORE       £1.50

A good tractor must be able
to handle all sorts of weather
Left: Ballicherry Farm
Above: Mains of Raddery

Left: Springfield

Keeping warm at Flowerburn Wood

Hoar frost and ash tree, Easter Culbo

Waterfalls at Fairy Glen (left) and Rosehaugh

Winter fieldscape, St Martins

Autumn fields, Munlochy

Left and above: Old croft, Bog of Cullicudden
Next Page: Gallow Hill and Moray Firth from Eathie

Above: Highland cattle,
Newhall
Left: Horse shaking off
snow, Upper Raddery
Right: Fairy Glen,
Rosemarkie

Fairy Glen, Rosemarkie, in autumn

Fairy Glen, Rosemarkie, in winter

Beech trees in spring, Raddery

Beech trees in winter, Raddery

# The Sky

THE Highlands of Scotland can boast some of the biggest skies in the world. The Black Isle has its share, especially after dark when the lack of light pollution means the dramatic colours of the Aurora Borealis – the Northern Lights – can sometimes be seen, or during the day when mountains and moisture combine to create lenticular clouds (see Page 72).

But even on an ordinary day there are some extraordinary sights to be seen above the Black Isle.

SIGHTINGS of the Northern Lights are not uncommon over the Black Isle. Generally they are witnessed more in winter, when the hours of darkness are increased, but they can be seen at any time of the year if conditions are favourable.

Two exceptional displays took place in November 2003. The photographs here were taken on the 20th, a week or two after an earlier display which I did not see. All photographs were taken on an early digital compact camera.

Andrew

# The Industry

ONE of the most unexpected sights for first-time visitors to the rural Black Isle is heavy industry, but the oil rigs in the Cromarty Firth are now as much a part of the landscape as dolphins and barley fields.

The oil yard at Nigg has fallen on hard times but Invergordon, across the firth, remains a major centre for the repair and refurbishment of rigs for the North Sea and beyond.

It is also a regular port of call for cruise liners – the deep waters which once made it an important anchorage for the Royal Navy mean even the biggest passenger ships can berth there safely.

Newhall Point on the Black Isle is a popular place for spectators to watch ships and rigs arrive and depart, often accompanied by the dolphins who enjoy riding vessels' bow waves.

Rigs can dwarf the village of Cromarty

The
industrial and
the natural
world in
harmony at
Cromarty
Firth

Above: Boats for work and play, Cromarty Firth
Right: Dolphins escort a ship past Fort George,
opposite Chanonry Point, on its way to Inverness

Left: Rural Black Isle and industrial Invergordon
This page: In summer, cruise liners are a common sight in the Cromarty Firth

Oil rigs can become a part of the landscape

# The Coast

Nowhere on the Black Isle is more than a few minutes from either the Moray Firth or the Cromarty Firth and echoes of the peninsula's maritime past are everywhere. Pleasure boats are now more likely to be seen than fishing vessels, but the big skies and dramatic views remain.

Above: Chanonry Lighthouse
Right: Beauly Firth from North Kessock

McFarquhar's Bed – Above: Fishing bothy and ruined salmon station
Right: Rock arches on the shore; Far Right: Land and sea from the cliff top

Westerly squall, Cromarty Harbour

At anchor, Cromarty Harbour

Left:
Cromarty
Bridge
Above:
Sunrise
from
Rosemarkie
Right:
Across
Udale Bay

Playtime on the beach at Rosemarkie

Summer at Fortrose Harbour

Left: Swans at dusk, Cromarty Firth
Top and right: Sunrise, Udale Bay
Above: Cromarty Firth dawn

# The Dolphins

CHANONRY Point near Fortrose is arguably the most important place in Europe, maybe further, for land-based dolphin watching. Tens of thousands of visitors come to the point every year for the chance to see the Moray Firth's most famous residents. On a good day, with an extra-low tide, the bottlenose dolphins come within a few feet of the shingle shoreline where they lie in wait to ambush salmon and sea trout en route to the rivers Ness and Beauly.

I have spent hours and hours watching these amazing animals and can honestly say that every time they leap feels like the first time. It's amazing, it's exciting and it never fails to make me smile. I have stood on the point beside people who maybe just came for the view and when a dolphin appears they say in amazement: "Did I just see a dolphin? Was that a dolphin? Oh my word that was a dolphin!" Of course, the dolphins don't always show up and they don't always leap or throw salmon in the air, but when

The road to Chanonry Point from Rosemarkie

they do it's a sight you will never forget – and that's a promise.

The Moray Firth dolphins are said to be the largest and most northerly bottlenose dolphins on earth. The Moray Firth can be very cold so the dolphins carry extra blubber as protection. To do this they eat lots of food and Chanonry Point is the perfect place to catch it. The huge sweeping bay that runs from Rosemarkie to Chanonry creates deep turbulent currents as the incoming tide races round the bay and hits the shelf just off the point, pushing water up and around like a huge washing machine. The dolphins lie in wait, using echolocation to find their meal, and they can often be seen racing across the surface like a torpedo when a fish is located. The sight of huge fish thrown high in the air is common.

Salmon and sea trout are the preferred choice of the dolphins but bass, mackerel and other shoal fish are also important parts of the extensive diet.

Each dolphin is unique and can be identified by markings on the dorsal fin. They are all individual in terms of their personality, too, with some more likely than others to leap, splash around and provide the kind of entertainment that has earned them their great reputation.

This book was put together to convey a feeling of what The Black Isle means to us. The Moray Firth dolphins, more that anything else, sum up my Black Isle. If you are lucky enough to visit, and lucky enough to see the dolphins at their finest, then you will understand.

James

Storm clouds over Chanonry Point

# The Wildlife

FOXES, pine martens, stoats, badgers, deer, red squirrels and a huge variety of birds are among the creatures that share the Black Isle with its human residents, and the area is believed to be one of the last strongholds of the most secretive of them all – the Scottish wildcat. Here are just a few of the creatures glimpsed in the fields, woodlands, gardens and sky of the Black Isle. There are many more, but that would take another book...

Facing page: Fox
Left: Common lizard
Right: Red squirrel

Roe deer

Female
pine
marten

Young
male pine
marten

Left:
Greylag
geese,
Easter
Culbo
Right:
Red kite
over
Leanaig

This page: Crested tit, Eathie (top); Young robin, Newhall (left); Dunlin, Chanonry Point (above)
Right: Flight of knot, Udale Bay

# The Photographers

Andrew Dowsett is a freelance photographer providing photographic and printing services for local businesses and artists. His work is varied but his greatest pleasure comes from recording landscapes and pictorial scenes close to home on the Black Isle and the shores of the Cromarty Firth where he has lived since 1986. He currently uses a Nikon D700 with 16-35mm, 50mm and 70-300mm lenses although many of his earlier photographs were taken on 35mm and medium format film cameras.

www.andrewdowsett.co.uk

James Alan Moore moved to The Black Isle in 2006 and was so amazed by the Moray Firth dolphins that he decided to take up photography. His passion has grown and developed to encompass a broader range of subjects and a particular interest in nature and landscape photography. All images were taken with a Canon 1D MKIII with a Canon 300mm lens and a Canon 40D with a 10-22mm lens.

www.jamesamoore.co.uk

Russell Turner is a journalist and author who swapped pen for camera when he discovered digital photography in 2006, the year before he moved to the Black Isle. In 2009 he became a Licentiate of the Royal Photographic Society, although he still considers himself very much a beginner. Landscape and wildlife photography are his greatest interests. He uses a Pentax K100D and two Pentax lenses: an 18-55mm and a 50-300mm.

www.russellturner.org

## The Photographs

*Introduction:* Cover AD, 3 RT, 4-7 AD
*Light:* 8 AD, 9 JM, 10 AD, 11 RT, 12 JM, 13 top AD bottom JM, 14-15 RT, 16 JM, 17 RT, 18-19 AD, 20 RT, 21 JM
*Villages:* 23 JM, 24-25 AD, 26 RT, 27 AD, 28 RT, 29 JM, 30-41 AD, 42-43 RT
*Land:* 44 AD, 45-46 JM, 47 AD, 48-56 AD, 57 JM, 58 AD, 59 JM, 60-61 AD, 62 JM, 64-69 AD

*Sky:* 70-75 AD
*Industry:* 76 JM, 77 AD, 78-80 AD, 81 JM, 82 RT, 83-85 AD
*Coast:* 86-87 JM, 88 RT, 89 top and bottom AD right RT, 90 AD, 91-93 JM, 94-97 AD
*Dolphins:* 98 AD, 99-105 JM. 106 RT
*Wildlife:* 108 JM, 109 left RT right JM, 110 JM, 111 RT, 112-3 JM, 114-5 RT, 116-7 AD, 118 top JM left RT right JM, 119 AD

*All the photographs are available for purchase. For information, contact the photographers through their websites.*